The
Essential
Guide
for Small
Group Leaders

BILL SEARCH

THE ESSENTIAL GUIDE FOR SMALL-GROUP LEADERS
From SmallGroups.com

Copyright © 2017
Christianity Today and William Search

Published by Christianity Today,
465 Gundersen Dr., Carol Stream, IL 60188

Printed in the U.S.A.

SmallGroups.com
ChristianityToday.org

Scripture taken from the Holy Bible, New International Version®, NIV®. Copyright © 1973, 1978, 1984, 2011 by Biblica, Inc.™ Used by permission of Zondervan. All rights reserved worldwide. www.zondervan.com

SMALLGROUPS.COM TEAM
Associate Publisher: Amy Jackson
Design: Jillian Hathaway
Marketing: Kristen Cloyd

SmallGroups.com

To Karyn, Maegan, Emma, and Jack.
You will always be my most important group.

Table of Contents

Acknowledgments

Thank you, Amy Jackson, for grabbing hold of this project and bringing it to fruition! Your excitement for it, your follow-up questions, and your gracious edits made this book a reality!

A big thanks to my girl, Maegan, for turning dozens of videos into a written transcript. You helped transform a series of training videos into something we can read.

This project began many years ago as a series of videos produced by Cary Meyer and filmed and edited by Rick Moore at Southeast Christian Church. I'm thankful to Cary and Rick for getting behind the video portion of this well before it became a book!

Thanks Steve Gladen for being an excellent mentor and friend. Your emphasis on what really works helped me avoid just being a groups philosopher and focus instead on helping small-group leaders succeed.

I am grateful for my wife, Karyn, who constantly encourages and lovingly supports me!

Most of all, I am thankful to Jesus Christ—my Savior and my friend.

Foreword

As our friendship has developed through the years, I have watched Bill wrestle with how to simplify small groups. He always asks what is really working? What is really helpful? What can help make stronger disciples? His first book, *Simple Small Groups*, did just that, and it's a good read!

In this new book, he aims at the core of a small-group ministry: the small-group leader. He approaches groups through the eyes of a small-group leader. What do leaders need? How can a leader develop and improve? How can leaders best care for the people in groups and enable each of them to pursue Christlikeness.

You will feel Bill's heart for you, the small-group leader, throughout this book. He strips away the chaff and focuses on creating a practical and helpful resource. With an easy to navigate format, helpful suggestions, and short sections, the aim of his book is to scratch where the leader itches. Every leader has challenges, and it's highly likely that the question or concern you have is addressed in the following pages.

Having trained tens of thousands of leaders throughout my 20 years at Saddleback Church, I know this resource will help you as a small-group leader or the leaders at your church!

STEVE GLADEN
Pastor of Small Groups, Saddleback Church
Author, *Leading Small Groups With Purpose* and *Small Groups With Purpose*

Introduction

I have a bookshelf full of books on small-group ministry, and I have found each one helpful in its own way. But let's be honest, most small-group leaders don't have time to read a book on small groups. Most barely have time to lead a group, much less explore the ins and outs of group ministry like ministry strategy, ministry administration, and various models of group ministry. Most group leaders simply want to know how to lead their group well!

This book is written for this kind of small-group leader. You'll find simple, clear answers to the questions you have. The content and the layout is presented so you can quickly and easily find the answers you need. To make this more accessible, it's written as lists and laid out like a manual. Maybe it's my blue-collar roots, but I like things that are simple, clear, and concise. I don't need stories and illustrations—I want action-oriented bullet points. There's no need to read this book straight through. Instead, use this book like a toolbox full of useful equipment. Flip to the sections you need when you need them.

I've been part of the small-group movement for more than 20 years serving in churches large and small. All small groups in all churches deal with many of the same issues:

- How do I start a healthy group?
- How do I build relationships within my group?
- How do I help people grow as Christ-followers?
- How do I help my group become more outward-focused?

Every group has struggles. Every group has its ups and downs. Every leader feels overwhelmed at some point. But here's the good news—the answers to your biggest leadership questions are pretty simple. There are easy steps you can take and simple principles you can apply that will solve the most common problems your group will encounter.

Section One:
Start Your New Group

18

How to Find and Recruit People for Your Group

Some churches have lists of people looking to join a group. But most don't. If you fall into that latter category, don't be discouraged. It's not terribly difficult to fill your group. Here's how:

1. **PRAY.**
   Ask God to help you find the right mix of people for your group.

2. **BE OPEN-MINDED.**
   Don't look for your idea of perfect people. Look for the right people. Every sports team is surprised by who turns out to be a great team member and who doesn't—so be willing to take a chance on others. You'll be surprised!

3. **MAKE A LIST.**
   Write down every name that comes to mind, even people you don't think will join the group. If you want 12 people, try to create a list of 20 people. Your list could include people you know from your church, who live in your neighborhood, or who work with you. Include anyone you'd like to have in your small group and anyone you think could benefit from a small group.

4. **FIND A PARTNER.**
   It's easier to lead if you have a partner. Start with the first person or couple on your list and work your way down. The first person or couple who agree to start the group with you can help you enlist others into the group.

5. **REPEAT.**
   Once you have a partner, go through steps 1-3 again.

6. **INVITE.**
    Email each person on the list and follow up with a phone call. An email might get lost in a spam folder, so don't assume an unanswered email is a "no." If you don't hear back from the person, pick up the phone or have a face-to-face conversation to invite potential group members.

7. **BE CLEAR.**
    When you invite, explain what a small group is and what you hope to accomplish by starting the group. (For a sample of what you can tell potential group members, see page 21.)

8. **SET A START DATE.**
    Usually the beginning of the fall, January, and early spring are good start dates. Avoid holidays and the summer when schedules are harder to align.

9. **SEND OUT A REMINDER.**
    Send out emails, texts, or Facebook messages the week before and again one day before your first meeting.

5 Things to Tell Potential Group Members

When you are forming a group, the first step is the invitation. It's vital that the invitation is clear, simple, and comprehensive. You certainly don't want potential members to feel you've baited them into an experience only to switch it once they are in your family room! Here are five key elements to communicate simply and clearly:

1. **FREQUENCY.**
   Is your group hoping to meet once a week? Twice a month? Before you send your first email or place your first call, nail this down.

2. **LENGTH.**
   Most groups meet for approximately two hours. That's enough time to build relationships and study God's Word. Be clear how long each gathering will last.

3. **DURATION.**
   Most leaders hope their group will feel like family and keep meeting indefinitely, but that's overwhelming to communicate to potential group members. It's wise to ask for a 10- to 12-week commitment with the expressed hope that the group stays together longer. Providing an easy escape at the 10- to 12- week mark will encourage people to give the group a try. And most people will stay with the group long after that.

4. **STUDY.**
   People come for content, but they stay for relationships. What topic will you explore? Most people feel stretched and overcommitted, so if you pitch your group as an opportunity to learn and grow, more people are likely to say "yes."

5. **PURPOSE.**
   Do you want your group to be a deep, disciple-making machine? A safe place for the spiritual seeker? A support group? Be clear up front. A seeker will feel overwhelmed in a group that is full of lifelong Bible students and the lifelong Christian might be bored in a seeker group. Let potential group members know what will be expected of them.

Conduct a Great First Meeting

The most important meeting in your small group is your first meeting! Each attendee will judge the future of the group on the first gathering. They will draw conclusions about the purpose of the group and the other attendees on the first gathering. Nail this and the group will do well. But if this meeting isn't strong, the group might not make it. It's worth the extra effort to make it great!

1. **PRAY.**
   Don't miss this step! Ask God to bless the meeting and to help everyone show up to the group.

2. **PREPARE THE ENVIRONMENT.**
   Arrange the furniture so that everyone has a seat and can see one another. Set the thermostat a little cooler than normal so that everyone is comfortable. Rooms heat up the more people are in them. Make sure you have good lighting so that people can read their Bibles and study materials and also see each other. An ambient mood is less important than the ability to see clearly. Remove any pets from the rooms you're using.

3. **MEET PEOPLE AT THE DOOR.**
   Greet them personally and make them feel welcome. Most of us struggle to remember names, so give everyone a name tag to take the pressure off. Everyone prefers to be called by their name rather than "pal," "dude," or "sport."

4. **SERVE REFRESHMENTS.**
   Simple finger foods, snacks, or a dessert help everyone relax. Don't overthink it and don't overdo it—simple is good!

5. **CIRCLE UP WITHIN THE FIRST 15 MINUTES.**
   It's important to start on time or the initial meeting will feel

awkward and poorly planned. If you wait for everyone to show up before you start, you may never start!

6. **START THE GROUP WITH AN ICEBREAKER.**
   Invite everyone to introduce themselves and use a fun icebreaker to help everyone relax. You might even want to do two or three icebreakers!

7. **END THE GROUP EARLY.**
   A good rule of thumb is to end 15 minutes before the official stop time and express your gratitude to those who came. Remind everyone of the time, date, and location of your next meeting. Be sure to end on time for your first few meetings! You want new members craving more time together not glancing at their watches. Eventually the relationships will sync up and you'll have a challenge ending on time, but during your first few gatherings, when members are still deciding if this group is for them, be sure to end on time or a little early. Honoring the time commitment communicates value to each group member.

8. **CLOSE THE GROUP IN PRAYER.**
   During the first meeting, don't take prayer requests. Save that for the next meeting. Instead, pray generally for your new group. Keep the prayer short and simple.

9. **CALL.**
   A few days after the first meeting, call everyone who came, thanking them for coming and reminding them about the details for the next meeting (where you will meet, time, and anything they need to bring).

Easy Icebreakers for New Groups

When your group is new, spend time getting to know each other. People don't care how much you know until they know how much you care. The most important thing you can do in the early season of your group is build the relationship connections within the group. The simplest way to accelerate that is through icebreakers, which are questions that are easy to answer with no right or wrong answers. Here are several simple, non-threatening icebreakers perfect for new groups:

1. If you were given a time machine and access to see any concert in the whole history of the world, who would you go see?

2. If you were trapped in a room for a week and could only have one movie with you, what would you choose to watch?

3. Choose three items from your wallet or purse that reveal something about you and share them with the group.

4. When you were a child, where was your favorite place to vacation? What did you like about it?

5. If you could meet any famous person from history (not mentioned in the Bible), who would it be and why?

6. If you could pursue any profession except what you do now, what would you do?

5 Simple Childcare Solutions

Every parent should be concerned for the safety and well-being of their children, including at small group. No book or ministry can tell a parent what to do, but here are some options for groups to provide care for the kids while the parents meet.

1. **PARENTS HIRE THEIR OWN BABYSITTER.**
   This is the easiest one with the best ratio of caregiver to child. Of course, this is also the most expensive option, so it can be a barrier to joining a group for some parents.

2. **INCLUDE THE CHILDREN.**
   You don't exclude kids from family reunions so why exclude them from your group? Just adjust your expectations. When kids are in the mix, the discussion may have to slow down to accommodate their input (and interruptions). You may also need to take more time to explain a Bible passage or a principle. You'll know it's worth the effort when you see growth in the next generation!

3. **ROTATE KID DUTY.**
   Each meeting, two adults can be on kid duty, watching the children in another area or room of the house. This should always be done in pairs so that adults have company and to provide added protection for the children. This allows the group to enjoy some kid-free time without having to pay a babysitter.

4. **HIRE A BABYSITTER (OR TWO) FOR THE SMALL GROUP.**
   The kids are looked after, the adults enjoy the discussion with minimal interruption, and no one goes broke as all parents pitch in to help.

5. **HAVE OLDER KIDS IN THE GROUP HELP WITH THE YOUNGER KIDS.**
   This one is a bit riskier. But if there are some responsible "tweeners" or teenagers, they may be able to watch over the younger kids. You might consider paying them a small amount each week, too.

Basic Ground Rules for Brand-New Groups

A good family has spoken and unspoken expectations, and a healthy small group is no different. We all have different ideas, however, of what some call "common sense." I always joke that "common sense isn't"—things commonly held aren't always sensible, and what I think is sensible isn't necessarily common. For this reason, lay out the ground rules in the first meeting. It's good to establish a covenant later on to make the ground rules official (see page 31), but in the very first meeting, it's enough just to cover the following:

1. **BE HERE PHYSICALLY.**
   Make attending the group a high priority and make every effort to be present.

2. **BE HERE EMOTIONALLY AND SPIRITUALLY.**
   Fully participate in the conversation and share what you really believe.

3. **PRACTICE RESPECT AND MUTUAL CONSIDERATION.**
   People don't care how much you know until they know how much you care. Let's demonstrate an appreciation for one another in the way we discuss different topics.

4. **SHARE OPINIONS AND CONVICTIONS WITH GRACE.**
   Some of us have very strong convictions. We can and should be true to those convictions, but let's not mimic the cable news opinionators in the way we approach one another. Let's season our conversations with grace.

5. **LEAVE POLITICS AND BUSINESS OUT.**
   Until you more fully know each other, avoid hot potatoes.

6. **THE BIBLE IS THE ULTIMATE AUTHORITY.**
   Experience, opinions, and popular culture all have something to teach us, but the Word of God is the foundation of a healthy group.

Create an Exceptional Group Covenant

Every group needs a set of operating rules. The business term SOP (standard operating procedure) refers to agreed-upon principles by which an organization hits maximum potential. Marriages have them, too: on their wedding day, a couple enters into a legally (and spiritually) binding covenant with one another. Whatever you call it—SOP, covenant, agreement, ground rules—every small group needs a set of agreed-upon principles to be healthy. Without this, the group won't live up to its potential. After your group has met a few times, create a document with these ground rules. Some groups print out a copy for each member, some have a party where everyone signs the paper, and others just read the covenant from time to time. Here are the big four covenant categories you'll need to cover:

1. **COMMITMENT.**
   Establish clear expectations for how often the group meets, the length of the meetings, and the general "life expectancy" of the group.

2. **CONFIDENTIALITY.**
   Make it clear that group members can trust one another with sensitive information. Group members want to know that what is said in the group will stay within the group. This allows them to speak truthfully.

3. **RESPECT.**
   Communicate how important it is to treat one another with honor and dignity. Remind group members to treat each other as they want to be treated.

4. **PURPOSE.**
   Clarify what the group is trying to accomplish. Decide why the group is meeting and what outcomes are expected.

5 Ways to Ruin a Brand-New Group

Any of these five problems have the potential to prematurely end a brand-new group. Allow any of these to fester, and it's likely the group will splinter apart.

1. **DO BUSINESS.**
   Don't use your group to add to your network marketing business or consider every new person in the group as a future client for your business.

2. **TALK POLITICS.**
   If you assume everyone shares your political convictions and belittle people who don't agree with you, your group won't last long.

3. **DEMAND TRANSPARENCY.**
   One surefire way to make everyone uncomfortable: force everyone to be open and transparent from day one. Let people warm up to the group over time rather than insist they share at a deep level.

4. **GET EMOTIONALLY UNHINGED.**
   Emotions are welcome in groups, but unrestrained, immature expressions will tank a new group.

5. **CONFESS YOUR BIGGEST SIN.**
   Sure, we've all got sin, but the first meeting might not be the time to confess. Especially if you turn to the person beside you and say, "You're next."

Address Inconsistent Attendance

Life is busy, and it's common to have someone missing at group meetings. You are not a failure as a leader if you don't achieve 100 percent attendance at every meeting. But if the same people always miss, or if group members don't let you know that they'll be gone, it may create an unhealthy group culture. Here are some ways to achieve more consistent attendance:

1. **SET THE GROUND RULES.**
   During the first several meetings, reaffirm the expectation that everyone should make every effort to be present at group meetings.

2. **PLAN AHEAD.**
   Put group meetings on the calendar and plan gatherings (and potential cancellations) in advance. Most busy people operate from a calendar, so get the group meetings on the calendar.

3. **ASK FOR ADVANCED WARNING WHEN SOMEONE KNOWS THEY WILL MISS.**
   Express the importance of notifying the group or leader when a group member is going to miss.

4. **BE THE "TRUANT" OFFICER.**
   If you have a no-show, call or text the missing member within 24 hours. This demonstrates your concern but also reminds the missing person that his or her absence was felt.

5. **GIVE MEMBERS AN OUT.**
   If you have a member who frequently misses, give him or her an opportunity to leave gracefully. When you talk to the person, explain that you understand that life is busy and full or obligations, and that you understand they may need to take a season off from the group. In reality, that "season" may be forever, but it's gentler to ask them in this way.

6. **REVIEW THE COVENANT.**
   Every six to nine months, revisit the covenant and remind group members of the importance of being physically present at group gatherings.

Pursue the No-Show

After the first few missed meetings, it's important to go after the no-show group member. Find out why he or she isn't attending and if there is anything you can do about it. Not everyone checks email regularly, and some emails get stuck in a spam folder, so I don't always trust email. When you have new people fall off the radar, do what you can to pursue them.

1. **KEEP AN EYE OUT.**
   Do you attend church together? Work together? Live near each other? Keep an eye out for the no-show. If you see them in person, don't judge or attack them. Instead, communicate your deep desire to help them connect to your group. If you never bump into them, pick up the phone.

2. **CALL.**
   After someone misses their first or second meeting, call the person, express that he or she was missed, and share the details of the next meeting. If you get a voicemail, leave your number. If the person doesn't call back, try again in a couple of days.

3. **FINAL WARNING.**
   When someone misses a third meeting, call again. If you get voicemail a second time, leave your number again. If they don't show up to the next meeting, move to step 4.

4. **GIVE THEM AN OUT.**
   If they still don't show, call one last time. Express that you missed the person at group, but add that you understand if things have come up and they aren't able to be part of the group. This will give them an easy way to say they're no longer able to attend. Then inform your coach or pastor.

Help! I'm Doing Everything!

When your group is new, it's common for everything to fall on your shoulders: hosting, leading, refreshments, follow-up. But after a few months, you should be sharing the load. Here's how:

1. **CAST VISION FOR SHARED OWNERSHIP.**
   Moses gave Joshua tasks, Jesus shared the ministry with his disciples, and Paul developed servants of the church. God never expected one person to do everything. In example after example in the Bible, we see shared ownership of the work to which God has called his people.

2. **ASK.**
   Simply invite members of your group to pitch in and help. Ask for willing volunteers to host or bring treats. Ask if someone would keep the prayer list up-to-date or perhaps lead the discussion. Send around a sign-up sheet with blanks for hosting, leading the discussion, and anything else you want help with. Keep sending it around and around until every blank is full.

3. **ASSIGN.**
   If asking doesn't work, assign various tasks. Ask specific people to do specific tasks based on their gifts, interests, and skills. They may not have seen themselves as good in this particular skill.

4. **ULTIMATUM.**
   If that doesn't work, be honest with your group. Recast the vision for how you all benefit when everyone pitches in. Explain that you can't lead if everything falls on you. Obviously, this is a last resort—but it clearly communicates that everyone needs to pitch in for a group to be a success.

Keep Your Spiritual Batteries Charged

A s leaders, it's our job to invest in others, and that requires us to keep our batteries charged. Many leaders, however, fail to invest in their own spiritual life as they lead. As a result, they grow spiritually dull. Here are five ways to prevent this from happening to you:

1. **START YOUR DAY IN PRAYER.**
   As soon as your feet hit the floor, thank God for the day. Find an approach that works for you—short prayers, long prayers, prayer journals, prayer reading. How you pray is less important than doing it consistently.

2. **READ A PORTION OF THE BIBLE EVERY DAY.**
   God reveals his will through his Word, so digest a portion of the Bible every day. Consider using Bible apps (such as YouVersion), The One Year Bible, or email devotionals to help you stay on course. Remember, conquering a system isn't the goal—hearing from God is.

3. **PARTICIPATE IN THE LIFE OF YOUR CHURCH.**
   Attend worship services weekly. How can you know what's happening with your church if you aren't there often? You should also serve regularly. Yes, leading a group is service, but engaging in other forms of serving will help form you holistically. And don't forget to work toward tithing to your church. When we tithe faithfully to God, he blesses us through meeting our needs, drawing us closer to him, and maturing us in the Lord. Pastor Rick Warren often says, "90 percent of your income with God's blessing will go further than 100 percent without it."

4. **WEAVE WORSHIP MUSIC INTO YOUR DAILY ROUTINE.**
   Use your daily commute to worship God. If you sing along, the drivers next to you will assume you're just talking on speaker phone.

5. **READ AN INSPIRING CHRISTIAN BOOK FOUR TIMES A YEAR.**
   Learn from faithful people of the past through Christian biographies, or challenge yourself with a Christian living book or a book on doctrine. If reading isn't your forte, try audio books.

How to Find a Coach

All group leaders need somebody who will invest in them, encourage them, and pray for them. In small-group circles we call these people "coaches." Some churches appoint a coach for each leader, but many do not. If you don't have a coach, here's what to look for and how to recruit one:

1. **A FAITHFUL PERSON.**
   Look for a person with a dynamic relationship with God who loves the church and the people of God. Avoid people who act pious and religious but lack a genuine spiritual life. People who have experienced God's grace exhibit humility, commitment, and an eagerness to continue growing.

2. **A JOYFUL PERSON.**
   You will pick up the characteristics of your coach. Look for a person who tackles the challenges of life with joy. God doesn't say we should always be happy, but he does say we should always be joyful. Avoid bitter complainers.

3. **AN ENCOURAGING PERSON.**
   Look for a person who passes out blessings, lifts others up, and seems to smile more than he or she frowns. Avoid critics, cynics, and snide people who always see the thorns on the rose without being willing to work toward change.

4. **SUGGEST A MEETING.**
   Schedule a coffee or lunch meeting and ask him or her to consider serving as your encourager and prayer supporter. Explain that you'd like to meet four to five times a year to talk through leadership and receive coaching. Just be warned: You may have to convince this person to coach you, since the best coaches rarely see themselves as qualified.

5. **SEEK THEIR COUNSEL.**
   Don't wait for the meeting. As issues come up, email, call, or text, and ask for tips on handling issues coming up in your group.

Section Two:
Develop Meaningful Relationships

Why You Should Be an Open Group

Some groups will always remain open to new attendees, while other groups will go through seasons where new people are welcome to join. Here are some indicators that it could be time to open up your group:

1. **SMALL.**
   If your small group is less than three people for a gender-specific group or less than eight people for a mixed/couples group, consider welcoming new people. If a group is too small when a member can't be present, then the discussion is lacking. Men's and women's groups are usually full at 6-8 people, and a mixed or couples group is usually full at 12-18. The reason it's important to cap the size of the group has much to do with the clock. If you have 12 members, each member has only five minutes per hour to share. More group members means less time for each person to share. Unfortunately, this usually means a few will dominate the entire meeting.

2. **AFTER A SEMESTER BREAK.**
   You don't have to be a student to think about semesters. The fall and the winter are prime seasons to welcome new people into your group.

3. **NEW CURRICULUM.**
   When you begin a new study, consider adding new people. It's easier to graft in newcomers on the first page than in the middle of the study.

4. **STUCK IN A RUT.**
   If your group has fallen into a rut, bringing new people in can spice up the group.

Why You Should Be a Closed Group

Nearly every group will go through seasons when they are not open to new members. This isn't a sign of selfishness or lack of evangelistic zeal—it's just one of the practical realities that visit all groups. Here are some reasons to be closed:

1. **SUPPORT GROUP.**
   Groups that require deep confidentiality where the insertion of a new person would cause insecurity should be closed.

2. **DIFFICULT ISSUES.**
   If the group is navigating conflict between members or a particularly challenging personality, adding new people won't help them or the group.

3. **PERSONAL CHALLENGES.**
   When a group member is facing an illness, a job loss, or another major issue, it's a good time to consider the group closed so the group can rally around this person.

4. **TAKING A BREAK.**
   Don't invite a new person to your last meeting before your three-month summer break. Or, if you're planning to end the group soon, don't invite new people. It's not fair to the new person to invite them to a group about to go on hiatus.

When Your Group Is Too Small

There is no ideal-sized group, but if a group is too small it can lack energy and diversity. Here's how to increase the size of your group.

1. **PRAY.**
   The simplest thing to do is often the last thing we do. Simply ask God, "Who should we invite to our group?" Then ask God to direct those people to you.

2. **REFLECT.**
   Why is your group small? Do you meet on a day or at a time when people are unavailable? Is the location inconvenient? Is the focus of the group unattractive? If your group has lost people, ask your coach or pastor to help assess why.

3. **MAKE A LIST.**
   Brainstorm names of potential group members. Pray over the list.

4. **STRATEGIZE.**
   Who should call the different people on the list? Will you invite everyone on the list or work your way down the list until you have the right number? Inviting everyone on your list could bring too many people. There's no right or wrong; just make a plan and get started! (For more on how to ask potential group members, see page 21.)

5. **WELCOME THE NEWBIE.**
   When a new person visits the group, make it a big deal. Wear name tags, greet them at the door, and give them a seat of honor. Weave in plenty of icebreakers and get-to-know-you games, and avoid inside jokes. New people don't want to feel like outsiders at a family picnic. When they officially join, throw a party!

6. **FOLLOW UP.**
   Ask the new attender what they like about the group and if they have any questions or concerns.

When Your Group Is Too Big

S ome insist there is an ideal size for small groups, but the truth is that groups of various sizes can serve different purposes. However, if you like a big group—I mean a really big group—you might find that your group will lose a sense of warmth and community because not everyone is able to share and participate. Here are a few things you can do to make a big group feel smaller:

1. **SUB-GROUP.**
   Stay together during the opening social time and teaching time (if there is such a time in your group), but form smaller groups of six to eight people during the discussion time and/ or prayer time. Then come back together for the conclusion of the group.

2. **BREAK INTO SMALLER PRAYER CIRCLES.**
   This will allow more people to share their prayer requests at a deeper level. Plus, more people can pray. The "bigger" requests that the whole group should know about can be shared with the whole group at the end.

3. **SPLIT THE GROUP IN HALF.**
   If your space allows, have one group in one room and the other group in another room. Make this a "permanent" arrangement, joining together only for social time, serving opportunities, and seasonal parties.

Split Your Group Without Creating Division

Sometimes even the best methods for making a big group feel smaller just don't work, and it's time to split the group into multiple groups that meet on their own. Some churches teach that every healthy small group should "give birth" to other small groups. The idea is that healthy groups are often adding more group members and eventually they simply become too big and need to split up to form two groups. While not all healthy groups will reach this point, it's important to be aware of some healthy strategies for splitting or multiplying into more groups. Here are six things you can do to maintain spiritual unity while dividing the group:

1. **MAKE IT A MATTER OF PRAYER.**
   Every time your group meets, weave a vision for group multiplication into the prayer time. For instance, pray that God would call members from within your group to start new groups. This invites God into the process and, through prayer, sows seeds within the members.

2. **INVITE THE COACH OR PASTOR.**
   Enlist an expert to help frame the vision for your group. Ask your coach or pastor to come to the group and share the vision for starting new groups from existing groups.

3. **IDENTIFY YOUR NEXT LEADER.**
   Every group has future leaders embedded in it. Sometimes we call them apprentices or potential leaders. You were probably the next leader in a group before you started leading. Invite that next leader to training events and ask your pastor or coach to meet with him or her.

4. **GET BIG.**
   Invite new people to your group until it gets awkwardly large.
   If the group outgrows the space, eventually the group might
   get a clue it's time to multiply.

5. **OFFER TO LEAVE.**
   Lead by example, and tell the group you're going to leave to
   start a new group but you can only take a few people with you.
   Explain your group will need a new leader since you can't lead
   two groups.

6. **CELEBRATE.**
   Launching a new group is a reason to throw a party, not a
   wake! Tell stories, eat great food, enjoy a cake, and have fun.

4 Ways to Care for Group Members

When done right, a small group provides such excellent support and care that church staff are seldom asked to provide pastoral care. Groups that do this well are there physically, emotionally, relationally, and spiritually during challenging times. There is a place for professional counselors and pastors, but a group can and should provide basic care for one another. When group members are facing a serious illness or issue, keep pastors and other appropriate church leaders informed about their condition. If there is a serious development, communicate that to the appropriate leaders.

1. **SHARE PERSONAL PRAYER REQUESTS.**
   It's great to pray for people outside of the group, but a healthy group prays for one another. Keep a prayer log and follow up on shared prayer requests.

2. **PROVIDE MEALS.**
   It's great to coordinate providing meals for families when a baby is born, after surgery, or during a time of extended illness.

3. **VISIT THE SICK.**
   Go to the hospital or visit at home. You don't have to have the right thing to say—showing up shows your support for your friends. Just don't stay too long!

4. **SEND NOTES, TEXT VERSES, AND COMMUNICATE CONCERN.**
   Whatever technology is appropriate for your group, use it to express your love. It's amazing how thoughtful words can boost the spirits.

Build Relationships During Meetings

M ost of us have full lives and packed schedules. Expecting groups to meet frequently outside of the normally scheduled group time is a challenge. The good news is you can use your group time to grow deeper ties within the group. Here are some simple things you can do:

1. **HOST A MEETING OF NOTHING BUT ICEBREAKERS.**
   Put aside the curriculum, grab a list of icebreakers, and host a meeting of nothing but questions. (See page 25 for some icebreakers to get you started.)

2. **SHARE A MEAL OR DESSERT EVERY TIME YOU MEET.**
   Brownies or burgers, there's nothing like food to create warmth and hospitality—and it's biblical! The early church broke bread together when they met.

3. **ROTATE HOSTING RESPONSIBILITIES.**
   Not only does this take pressure off of one person, but it also helps your group get to know each other better. When people open their home or apartment, they are sharing insight into who they are, what they value, and maybe even an odd collection or two!

4. **GIVE EVERYONE A JOB.**
   When each person feels some ownership of the group, the walls come down and the relationship ties grow stronger. Identify people to be the beverage and food coordinator, the prayer list coordinator, the Facebook page keeper, the social coordinator, and more. There is no end to the roles a group member can play. (For more on this topic, see page 39.)

5. **CARVE OUT TIME FOR PRAYER.**
   When group members share their prayer requests and have

the opportunity to pray for one another, they are building stronger bonds. (For ideas for group prayer, see pages 119 and 121.)

6. **SHARE YOUR TESTIMONY.**
Each week have a group member share his or her 15-minute spiritual biography, including the ups and downs, key influencers, special moments, and personality shapers. (See page 101 for tips on doing this well.)

Build Relationships Outside of Meetings

The closer the connections, the more genuine the discussion. You can accelerate the depth of relationships exponentially if you spend additional time together outside of the normal group meeting time.

1. **ATTEND CHURCH TOGETHER.**
   Meet before service, sit together, and hang out in the lobby after the service. Introduce your group to your friends and vice versa.

2. **SERVE AT CHURCH TOGETHER.**
   Turn your small group into a serving team and you'll double the time you enjoy together. You could rock babies, pass out bulletins, or welcome newcomers.

3. **GO OUT TOGETHER.**
   Enjoy dessert, coffee, dinner, shopping, a show, the theater, or a sporting event. There is no shortage of great options.

4. **PLAN A ROAD TRIP.**
   Start with a one-day or weekend trip. Carpool so you have fun together on the journey. Stay up late, play games, and build memories.

5. **GO ON A MISSION TRIP TOGETHER.**
   In the states or overseas, if your group serves on a mission trip together, you will forge a deep connection.

6. **CELEBRATE HOLIDAYS TOGETHER.**
   As your group becomes family, do the things a family does: carve pumpkins, decorate cookies, and dye Easter eggs.

Healthy Ways to Deal with Group Conflict

From time to time group members rub each other the wrong way. Our temptation is to ignore, suppress, or take sides in the conflict. But leaders are called to help group members work through the issues together, not hide from them. Here's how you can do that:

1. **STUDY BIBLE VERSES ON CONFLICT RESOLUTION TOGETHER.**
   Two key passages worth your focus are Matthew 18:15–17 and Galatians 6:1.

2. **IDENTIFY THE UNDERLYING ISSUE.**
   Like a massive iceberg that barely rises above the surface of the water, many of the issues that surface have a more significant component that needs to be addressed. Figure that out.

3. **INVOLVE ONLY THE PEOPLE IN CONFLICT.**
   Unless the whole group is embroiled in the issue, keep communication limited to the parties directly involved.

4. **AVOID GOSSIP.**
   Do not debrief the situation with others—even as a prayer request.

5. **ASK THE PARTIES INVOLVED TO MEET AND WORK IT OUT.**
   Unless needed, don't play judge or jury. Many conflicts can be worked through by those affected.

6. **SEEK INPUT FROM YOUR COACH OR PASTOR IF THE ISSUE ISN'T EASILY RESOLVED.**
   Seek wisdom from the right church official only if the matter requires more attention.

6 Group Killers to Avoid

No matter how strong the group, it can be undermined by some common problems. But address these common challenges, and you will enjoy much more time together.

1. **INCONSISTENT ATTENDANCE.**
   When people catch on that this group isn't a priority, everyone begins skipping out. So remind everyone to be a regular contributor to the group and expect solid attendance. Point to your covenant to remind your group members about this expectation.

2. **AWKWARD PERSONALITIES.**
   You can't simply ignore members who are insensitive toward the thoughts and feelings of others, who are rude, who have poor manners, or who require extra grace. Work with them to be participants and not stand-outs. (For tips on handling specific "odd" people, see pages 71 and 75.)

3. **SURFACE-LEVEL SHARING.**
   People who give cliché answers and ride the surface create an atmosphere of distrust. Model what you want to see. Be open, honest, and vulnerable, and challenge everyone else to do the same.

4. **BAD CURRICULUM.**
   Curriculum that is tedious, boring, or doesn't connect with the group can kill groups fast. If the material can be fixed by some edits, then add questions or adapt for your group. Otherwise, dump it and get new material. Be sure to communicate with your coach or pastor and ask for suggestions. (For tips on choosing great curriculum, see pages 111 and 113.)

5. **HOLIDAYS AND SUMMER BREAKS.**
   Respect the season and don't try to motor through. If people can't make it, take a break! Before you do, though, plan the next group gathering and get it on the calendar. During extended breaks (like summer and Christmas), plan to get together for a social event or a service outing at least once.

6. **SELF-ABSORBED MEMBERS.**
   Complainers who don't give or serve can quickly kill a group. Study the Great Commission (Matthew 28:18–20) together to inspire people to contribute. Challenge each person in the group to commit to an area of service. (For tips on nixing unhelpful complaining from your group, see page 69.)

Nix Negativity from Your Group

Often those who complain the loudest give and serve the least. A spirit of complaint is the enemy of mission. A group that adopts a negative overtone shows that they have become inward-focused and have lost a proper perspective. Here are some things you can do to change the tone:

1. **MAKE A LIST.**
   Create a list as a group of all the things you are grateful for. It's hard to complain when you're focusing on the good things in life.

2. **THANK YOU.**
   Pass out blank cards and ask everyone to take a few minutes and write a thank-you note to someone serving at church—an usher, a children's or youth worker, a worship leader—who they have noticed doing a good job.

3. **ADOPT A MINISTRY OR MISSIONARY.**
   Focus on people making a positive difference, and you'll be more positive, too.

4. **FIND SOLUTIONS.**
   If the same complaints keep showing up, brainstorm solutions to the problem. Remember, one solution might be to accept the situation as it is and ask for God's peace.

5. **PRAY.**
   Every time someone complains, stop what you're doing and invite the complainer to lead the group in prayer for that issue. Turn it over to God.

6. **CONFRONT.**
   Simply call out the complaint for what it is and ask the group to move forward on more productive endeavors.

Address Challenging Personalities

John Ortberg rightly says, "Everybody's normal until you get to know them." As the old saying goes, "In every group there is a challenging person, and if you don't know who it is, the person might be you!" Here are some of the common personalities that might show up in your group and how you can help. In each case, you need to develop a strategy to help them grow as a follower of Christ without letting them drag down your group.

1. **THE POLITICAL JUNKIE.**
   She assumes that everyone shares her political leanings and considers everyone who doesn't either an enemy or a fool to be corrected. She can be accidentally (and sometimes purposely) offensive.

   Strategy: Explain that your group is a place for everyone to build relationships, grow in their faith, and embrace the mission of God—and politics should stay in the driveway. People from all political parties and persuasions are welcome in your group.

2. **THE PHARISEE.**
   Like the Pharisees in the Gospels, he knows the words of the Bible very well but misses the point. He's overly pious and judgmental.

   Strategy: Remind him that a group isn't for perfect people (like the Pharisee thinks he is) but for people who are striving to grow in their faith.

3. **THE EGOMANIAC.**
   Everything—and I mean everything—somehow turns into a story about her. She can't share attention with anyone.

Strategy: Talk to her. Develop a plan that gets her involved in helping you include everyone. Ask her to help draw out others by asking questions that spark more discussion.

4. **THE NETWORK BUILDER.**
   You get the strange sensation that he joined the group to sell products or build his personal pyramid. At some point, he will ask you what you'd do with $5,000 extra a month.

   Strategy: Remind him that the group is not for recruiting, selling, or pushing our business on others. You can point to your covenant or ground rules for support.

5. **THE ILLUMINATI.**
   She believes every conspiracy theory passed around on the Internet, and she pushes these on your group members.

   Strategy: It's a free country and you can embrace any conspiracy theory you want, but the group needs to stick with the Bible and remember Jesus is the hope of the world. And since that is true, we don't need to live in fear. Jesus is for us!

6. **THE CRYPTIC.**
   Everything he says is mysterious and hard to understand. He never gives a straight answer, and he never asks a direct question.

   Strategy: Every time he says something or asks something that isn't clear, simply ask, "Can you say that in simpler terms? I don't quite understand what you're getting at."

7. **THE EMOTIONAL BLACK HOLE.**
   She dominates the prayer time with her extensive list of needs that are beyond the scope of the group.

Strategy: Explain to her that we all have struggles, and while some things she faces might be more extreme, we all need to support one another. Also remind her that your group is not a "support" group (unless that is the purpose of your group, of course). And since it's not that, you can't shut down the group to listen to her struggles.

8. **THE BOSS.**
   He may not be the official leader, but he sure acts like it. He speaks with authority (even when he doesn't have any) and is very sure of his opinions.

   Strategy: If he has genuine leadership gifts and a growing faith, invite him to be your apprentice and give him meaningful tasks that will engage his leadership gift. If he's just "bossy" and doesn't possess leadership gifts, or if he's spiritually immature, have a gentle conversation with him and remind him of the group rules.

9. **THE CONTRARIAN.**
   She lives to argue. She's listening for any mistake and jumps on it. She parses every word.

   Strategy: Well-behaved contrarians can help a group think outside the box. When she's mature, she's a gift to the group, as she makes every discussion more interesting. An immature contrarian is argumentative, rude, and combative. Outside of the meeting, remind her of the covenant and ground rules.

10. **THE STORY TOPPER.**
    The Topper is often a champion storyteller. At his best, he creates a fun space for everyone to tell stories about real (and exaggerated) life. At his worst, he competes for the best, most interesting, and grandest story, creating a competitive envi-

ronment that closes down the group.

Strategy: Have a gentle conversation with him if he gets out of line, and ask him how you can help signal to him when he's getting out of line.

11. **THE WANDERER.**
She's usually loveable and fun but she will take your group down many a rabbit trail if you let her. The curriculum is an optional map that she likes to ignore.

Strategy: At her best, she can improve discussions by carving conversational pathways that make the curriculum better. But she can also divert your group from accomplishing its purpose. To keep things on track, you might need to say, "That is an interesting question, but let's hold that for later and move along with these questions for now."

12. **THE COMEDIAN.**
Everything is a joke or an opportunity to make a joke. When he's at his best, he lightens the mood and puts a smile on every face. At his worst, he won't let anything serious invade the group, which halts deeper discussion.

Strategy: Laugh when appropriate, but keep the train moving forward. If he becomes too distracting, have a private conversation with him.

Dealing with Weird People

Some people lack self-awareness. They don't realize their behavior is having a negative impact on others. What are the right steps to help them understand how their behavior is affecting the group?

1. **START WITH LOVE.**
   You need to love the person enough to see their potential. Love should guide you to deal with the situation and not simply ignore it.

2. **PRAY FOR THEM.**
   Every person is made in the image of God. Every person is someone for whom Christ died. God loves them and so should we. Pray, "Dear God, help me see my friend as you see them."

3. **DON'T KICK THEM OUT.**
   Resist the urge to exclude them. God put them in your group for a purpose. Unless they are absolutely destroying your group, start out by trying to help them.

4. **HAVE A PRIVATE CONVERSATION.**
   Gently pull them aside. Invite them for coffee or lunch. Get to know them as a person. Don't confront in the group—you don't want to publicly embarrass the person.

5. **HELP THEM SEE HOW THEIR BEHAVIOR IMPACTS OTHERS.**
   Sometimes people know about their quirks, and sometimes they don't. Regardless, most don't realize how their behavior impacts the rest of the group. By lovingly pointing this out, most people will be motivated to work on the issue.

6. **ENLIST THEM IN A SOLUTION.**
   Ask how you can help them. What cue can you use in the

group that will alert the offender without publicly embarrassing them?

7. **FOCUS ON THE MISSION OF THE GROUP.**
   By reminding people that the purpose of the group is to help every member of the group and not just them, you help them not to take it personally. As you invite them to focus on others, you help them grow spiritually and relationally.

Engage in Confrontation

No one is perfect, and a group is the perfect place for imperfect people to belong. But, we shouldn't stay that way—we should challenge each other to become more like Christ. So how do we engage in challenging conversations? Here are some helpful steps to make it a "care-frontation":

1. **START WITH PRAYER.**
   Ask God for wisdom and for a pure heart and right motives. Ask that God would soften your friend's heart so that he or she is prepared to receive the conversation.

2. **SEEK INPUT FROM YOUR COACH.**
   Talk through the issue or concern with your coach or pastor. Don't turn to others in the group or seek out another friend in church—that's gossip. Seeking wisdom from those God has put in authority is the right channel.

3. **HAVE A FACE-TO-FACE CONVERSATION.**
   Meet person to person—do not engage in difficult conversations over the phone or via email, text, or letter.

4. **ASK FOR PERMISSION TO SHARE SOME OBSERVATIONS ABOUT THEM.**
   If they give you permission, share your observations with them. For example, "I've noticed that you have a tendency to interrupt others. Do you notice that, too? Has anyone ever brought that to your attention before?"

5. **USE THE "SANDWICH" TECHNIQUE.**
   "Sandwich" the concern between praise, encouragement, or affirmation. Encourage twice as much as you confront. For instance, "I love the heart and passion you bring to our discussions. I have noticed that you have a tendency to interrupt

others. Do you notice that, too? You often draw out such great observations, so I don't want you to hear criticism."

6. **FOCUS ON THE ISSUE.**
Do not attack the person, but address the issue. Talk only about the situation at hand.

7. **BE DIRECT, BUT NOT BLUNT.**
Don't beat around the bush and hope they catch on. Speak clearly and concisely, but don't be rude. Confront the way you would want to be confronted.

8. **ASK FOR A RESPONSE.**
It's very possible that they will affirm what you have observed. If so, ask how you can help.

9. **FOLLOW UP WITH ENCOURAGEMENT.**
Drop a note, a text, or an email reminding your friend of your love for them.

When It's Time to Show a Group Member the Door

The last resort is expulsion, but sometimes it's necessary for the health of the person and of the group. God accepts us as we are—but he won't let us stay that way. We all have the capacity to change and become the very best version of the person God intends for us to be. But members who refuse to work on issues that have a negative impact on the group will need to go. Never rush into this decision, and engage in many conversations before you take this drastic step. Seek the input of your coach or pastor and involve the members of the group when the time is right. (For more, see page 81.) Here are some of the particularly toxic people that need to leave if they won't accept help from the group:

1. **THE NO-SHOW.**
   The perpetual no-show who promises to come then cancels at the last minute (or worse, just doesn't show up) can have a dire impact on your group. People who won't commit—or over-commit—can inspire others to attend at their leisure. It won't take long for this to hurt your group.

2. **"IT'S ALL ABOUT ME."**
   People who insist on being the center of attention, who dominate every discussion, and who barely come up for air have to be dealt with. If they refuse to change, they need to go, or your other group members will leave.

3. **THE RUDE MEMBER.**
   With complete inconsideration for others, the rude member seems to thrive on offending others. He hurts feelings as a sport. If he won't work on it, he has to go.

4. **THE CHURCH LADY.**
   Many years ago, actor Dana Carvey created a hilarious character on *Saturday Night Live* known as the Church Lady. She thrived on putting others down as she exalted her own pious ways. Modern-day church ladies and church guys aren't funny. They kill groups.

How to Ask a Member to Leave the Group

On very rare occasions you may be called upon to ask a group member to leave the group. This task is to be entered into with deep prayer and consideration. Ultimately, you must do what is best for the group and what is best for the offending group member. Here are some suggestions for doing this tough task with grace and truth:

1. **KNOW THE ISSUE.**
   Understand exactly why you have to ask the member to leave the group. Is it spotty attendance? The unwillingness to work on previously articulated issues? Make sure you are clear.

2. **SEEK WISDOM FROM YOUR PASTOR OR COACH.**
   Since you are under the authority of a coach or pastor, act under their instruction. This protects you and your group if the member becomes irate.

3. **HAVE A PRIVATE CONVERSATION.**
   Explain to the person why they can't be part of your group. (For more, see page 79.) It's best to have this conversation face-to-face. The next best option is over the phone. Text and email are the very last resort.

4. **ARTICULATE EXPECTATIONS AND NEXT STEPS.**
   Is this a permanent dismissal, or a temporary one until the member works on the issue?

5. **POINT THEM FORWARD.**
   Refer them to a pastor for their next connection opportunity. Perhaps you've been forced to remove them due to attendance issues. If that's the case, perhaps a different group will cure the problem. If they have particular needs and require a support group format, refer them to their next spiritual step.

6. **BRING IN THE GROUP.**
   Inform the group after you have talked with the person. Remind them that you all still love the former member and to treat the person with love and dignity.

How to Energize a Worn-Out Group

Even the most exciting group can lose energy over time. Just because a group isn't as thrilling as it once was doesn't mean it has to end. It might just need a tune-up. Here are some suggestions for re-igniting the group relationships:

1. **BUILD A NEW COVENANT.**
   Take the old covenant and tear it up. Have a meeting dedicated to crafting a new group covenant and articulate what you want to see happen in the group.

2. **SWITCH IT UP.**
   Meeting in the same location week after week? Move to a new space. Using video? Switch to a study guide. Using only study guides? Switch to video.

3. **RETREAT.**
   Take a weekend away as a group and establish new goals for the group. (See "Plan a One-Day Retreat" on SmallGroups.com for ideas.)

4. **ADD NEW PEOPLE.**
   Fresh blood can infuse new energy.

5. **SERVE FOR A SEASON.**
   Instead of the typical group format, become a serving team for a season and bond over the task at hand. Volunteer in the nursery or with children's ministry, join the greeter or usher team, or volunteer with grounds and maintenance. As your group serves shoulder-to-shoulder, you will find new appreciation for each other.

6. **ASK THE EXPERT.**
   Invite a guest to teach or lead the group for a couple of sessions, or invite in guest speakers to teach a specific topic of

interest to the group. Brainstorm questions, give them to your pastor, and invite your pastor to a gathering to teach through the questions.

7. **HOT SEAT.**
   Each week rotate a group member to the "hot seat" and focus the whole meeting on getting to know them. Ask the person to come prepared with photos and mementos for a show-and-tell. You'll be surprised by what you learn—even from people you think you know well.

How to Know When It's Time to End Your Group

All groups run their course. Your group may last two years or ten years, but at some point it's time to call it quits. Here's how to know if it's time to bring your group to a close:

1. **ATTENDANCE DROPS OFF.**
   Attendance drops off as people find better things to do.

2. **THE GROUP FEELS FLAT.**
   The discussion is flat, the passion is gone, and it seems like joy has left the group. People stay because they are committed or because of the routine, but not because they are excited to be together.

3. **NOTHING WORKS.**
   You've tried to energize the group but it still lacks energy.

4. **YOU'VE GONE AS FAR AS YOU CAN GO.**
   Everyone seems to have gone as far as they are willing to go with the group. The transparency, confrontation, and confession are non-existent. Spiritual growth has ceased.

5. **NEGATIVITY RULES.**
   Whining and complaining are the norm.

6. **NATURAL TRANSITIONS CHANGE THE DYNAMIC.**
   When half of the singles group gets married, it might be time to end the group. When half of the young couples group starts having babies, it might be time. When half the couples group retires, it might be time. Natural transitions can be exciting times to celebrate and release.

How to End Your Group

If you've decided to end your group, it's time to celebrate what God has done in the group and close this chapter. Here's how to do that well:

1. **UNDERSTAND ALL GROUPS—NO MATTER HOW GREAT—COME TO A NATURAL END.**
   Realize you are not a bad leader, and your group is not a bad group. Every group ends, so recognize the season of ending and celebrate it.

2. **GET INPUT FROM GROUP MEMBERS.**
   Float the idea of ending to your group and get their opinion. If the majority says "yes," it's time to wind it down. If the majority says "no," involve your group coach or pastor to talk it through.

3. **ASK EVERYONE TO MAKE A PERSONAL PLAN.**
   Get options from your coach or pastor and share those with your group members. Will everyone join different groups? Take a season off from groups?

4. **PLAN A FINAL MEETING AND PUT IT ON THE CALENDAR.**
   Treat it like a party, and end with a bang. Invite former group members, share a meal, and swap stories about the impact of the group on your lives.

5. **END THE GROUP IN A PRAYER CIRCLE.**
   Thank God for all that has happened in your group, and pray for each other as you begin this new chapter.

6. **DON'T FORGET TO TELL YOUR PASTOR OR SMALL-GROUP COACH THAT YOUR GROUP HAS ENDED.**
   They may want to celebrate the group in a special way. If nothing else, they'll want to remove your group from any small-group sign-up materials.

Section Three:
Focus on Growth and Transformation

Help People Grow During Meetings

A group is supposed to help us grow deeply in our faith. What are some things we can do that will help each person take that next spiritual step?

1. **KEEP THE BIBLE CENTRAL IN THE DISCUSSION.**
   Personal opinions and ideas are part of the discussion, but God's Word is inspired and useful for changing lives. The apostle Paul wrote, "All Scripture is God-breathed and is useful for teaching, rebuking, correcting and training in righteousness, so that the servant of God may be thoroughly equipped for every good work" (2 Timothy 3:16–17). So, keep the Bible in its proper position.

2. **INCLUDE EVERYONE IN THE DISCUSSION.**
   Encourage each person to say what they really believe and not what they think the group wants to hear. Before we can grow, we have to admit where we are.

3. **ASK EACH GROUP MEMBER TO LEAD THE DISCUSSION.**
   When we are forced to explore a topic, prepare for a discussion, and lead others, we inevitably put more thought and prayer into it. As a result, leading others helps us grow. Even new and non-believing members can learn and teach something! If you have a new or non-believing member, you may start with a small section or assignment and ask them to lead that portion.

4. **TWICE A YEAR, SET ASIDE A MEETING TO SET PERSONAL SPIRITUAL GOALS.**
   Challenge each group member to identify and share their next spiritual step. Discuss how you can support one another in these goals.

Lead Great Discussions

The heartbeat of a great group meeting is an interesting discussion. How can you engage your members and draw out thoughtful responses? Here are several suggestions:

1. **KNOW THE POINT.**
   Before you begin the discussion, know the big idea that is driving the study that week.

2. **START WITH AN ICEBREAKER.**
   Help everyone relax and enter the conversation by asking an interesting question that everyone can answer. A good icebreaker question doesn't have a right answer. (For ideas, see page 25.)

3. **CREATE A SAFE ENVIRONMENT WHERE PEOPLE CAN SHARE WHAT THEY BELIEVE.**
   It takes courage to be honest and share at the heart level. Encourage and applaud vulnerable sharing.

4. **STAY ON COURSE AND BE FLEXIBLE.**
   Rabbit trails, irrelevant stories, and random humor can be fun and create shared memories. But when they take the group completely off course, they are not helpful.

5. **INVOLVE EVERYONE IN THE DISCUSSION.**
   A healthy group encourages everyone to speak up and share their thoughts. It might require that you quiet some and invite others in. (See pages 71, 75, and 99 for how to do this.)

6. **USE SPACE WELL.**
   Make sure everyone has a place to sit, is comfortable and free of distractions, and can see one another. Set chairs in a circle—or as close to a circle as you can get.

Ask Great Questions

There's nothing worse than a dud of a discussion. How do you prevent awkward silence? It's all about preparation and attitude. Here are some tips for asking great discussion questions:

1. **GET FAMILIAR WITH THE STUDY OR DISCUSSION GUIDE.**
   Read the questions out loud before the group meets. As you read them, consider how you would answer them. If they don't make sense to you or seem too simple, fix the questions so they will work in your group. Adapting and rewording questions is a discussion-saver!

2. **ASK OPEN-ENDED QUESTIONS.**
   If any question can be answered with "yes," "no," or a single word, don't ask it. If it can't be avoided, add, "Why did you answer that way?"

3. **IT'S ALL ABOUT THE "WHAT," "SO WHAT," AND "NOW WHAT."**
   What is the study all about? So what—why is this important? Now what do we do with it? A good discussion works through all three of those questions.

4. **AVOID QUESTIONS THAT FISH FOR "JUST THE RIGHT ANSWER."**
   Yes, there are right and wrong answers, but if the group members sense there is just one answer, very few will speak up out of fear of being wrong.

5. **DON'T CELEBRATE THE "RIGHT ANSWER."**
   This is the same as number 4 except you throw a party when you hear the answer you want. Celebrate the right answer and you will shut down future discussion.

6. **DON'T ANSWER YOUR OWN QUESTIONS.**
   If no one responds to a question, then ask a follow-up, "Did that question make sense?" Silence might be an indicator that group members are thinking, or it might be an indicator that the question needs to be reworded. Asking this follow-up question will help you know which is true.

7. **DON'T JUDGE SOMEONE'S ANSWER.**
   You might hear some doozies, but resist the urge to correct others. Instead, ask follow-up questions and seek more replies, like "Where do you see that in Scripture?" or "What do the rest of you think about that?"

Develop the Habit of Active Listening

Many people don't really listen—they just pause until it's their turn to talk. But leading a group means learning to listen. It's by listening to others that we understand who they are, what they believe, and how they relate to God. As a group leader, it's essential that you learn to listen so that you can better shepherd your group. Here are some helpful tips:

1. **MAKE EYE CONTACT.**
   Look at the person speaking. Ignore distractions. Let the person know you are paying attention.

2. **RESIST THE URGE TO INTERRUPT, STORY TOP, OR MAKE A JOKE.**
   These can make the environment unsafe and squelch deep sharing.

3. **ASK FOLLOW-UP QUESTIONS TO DRAW OUT MORE.**
   Asking additional questions honors the sharer and deepens the group's understanding of what is being shared. Ask, "Can you explain that again?" "What did you do next?" or, "Was that as challenging as it sounds?"

4. **RESTATE WHAT WAS SHARED.**
   Put the person's comment in your own words and ask if that's what they meant.

5. **ENCOURAGE EVERYONE TO STAY ENGAGED.**
   If other group members aren't paying attention, say something like, "Bob, can you repeat that so we can all hear it? Let's all give Bob our attention—this is important."

6. **THANK THEM FOR THEIR CONTRIBUTION.**
   This honors the sharer and encourages others to share at a deeper lever.

Help Group Members Open Up

We all face various challenges in life. But most of us want others to think we can handle it. So rather than seek input and prayer, we often hold in the hard things. A group, however, is the ideal place to receive support and encouragement—if you're courageous enough to step out. Here are some simple steps to deepen the level of sharing in your group:

1. **START WITH REALISTIC EXPECTATIONS.**
   Don't expect too much too soon. It often takes several months before group members are comfortable sharing at a deep level.

2. **MODEL THE WAY.**
   The group will follow your lead—they will mimic what they see and hear from you. Share honestly about things that are hard for you. Don't dramatize the challenges in your life, but don't minimize them, either.

3. **CREATE A SAFE, NON-JUDGMENTAL ENVIRONMENT.**
   It takes a lot of courage to share hurts and struggles with a group. Make it easier by shutting down any judgmental comments.

4. **DON'T TRY TO FIX OR SOLVE PROBLEMS.**
   There will be time later to brainstorm solutions—but most challenges aren't solved with a cliché sentiment and a quick prayer. For now, affirm people for sharing and show empathy.

5. **THANK EACH PERSON WHO SHARES.**
   Thank them for taking a risk and sharing vulnerably. Express your gratitude for your group member's openness.

6. **DON'T INSIST THAT EVERYONE OPENS UP.**
   A safe environment means freedom to be open and freedom to be quiet. Don't force anyone to share.

7. **TAKE A MOMENT TO PRAY.**
   Many of these deeper matters will come up during the prayer time, naturally leading to a time of prayer. But if something is shared during the discussion time, take a moment to pray over your friend.

Share Your Testimony

A key to understanding the members of your group is knowing their spiritual story. A testimony is not a biography—the focus is on the spiritual high points and low points of a person's life. If you want to grow relationally deep as a group, try this:

1. **SET THE TIMER.**
   Explain that the goal is to give a short testimony. Set the timer for a specific amount of time, and let everyone know that they will be timed. I like to do four-minute testimonies so that more people can share in one meeting. A short duration also reduces the tension for the person who hates being the center of attention. It's okay to have a laugh over the seemingly impossible amount of time.

2. **PASS OUT INDEX CARDS.**
   Put a dot on the far left representing your birth and a dot on the far right representing today. Then draw a line connecting the two. This is your spiritual journey.

3. **HIGHLIGHTS ONLY, PLEASE.**
   Share just a few sentences about family of origin and basic upbringing. Then identify three or four key highlights along your journey. If you're a Christian, be sure to include when you became a Christian.

4. **DON'T GIVE YOUR BIO.**
   A biography is your life story, but a testimony is much more focused. Sharing a 4-minute testimony gives just 60-90 seconds each for 3 to 4 significant events that had a big impact on you spiritually.

5. **MAKE IT SAFE.**
   Remind your group that this is a judgment-free zone. If you

learn that someone in your group hasn't yet become a Christian, be glad they are in your group. God has a plan for them (and you)!

6. **NO INTERRUPTIONS ALLOWED.**
   Time is precious, so save questions for after the person has shared.

7. **CLOSE WITH GRATITUDE.**
   Thank everyone for their openness and vulnerability. It's not easy to do what your group just did!

Create a Safe Environment to Confess Sin

The Bible instructs us to confess our sins to each other (James 5:16). This does not mean that every group should expect confession of sin to be a regular feature of the group. If your group has been meeting for several months and has grown close, confession is a beautiful part of a strong group. Here's how to encourage it:

1. **STUDY WHAT THE BIBLE SAYS ABOUT CONFESSION.**
   Read relevant passages and discuss together the role of confession in your group. Start with James 5:16, Ephesians 4:32, Romans 3:10–23, and Leviticus 5:1–6.

2. **BE REALISTIC.**
   Your group members may embrace this or they may not. Some groups take several months or a couple of years to experience genuine confession—and some never do. It's not a sign of group success or failure.

3. **SET THE TONE.**
   Others will follow the example you set. If you want to see confession in your group, then be the first to confess.

4. **CREATE A SAFE, NON-JUDGMENTAL ENVIRONMENT.**
   Don't interrupt, don't blame, and don't minimize or maximize the sin confessed.

5. **DON'T ABSOLVE SINS.**
   Only God can forgive sins. We can affirm that God will forgive us, but sin is not ours to forgive. That belongs to God.

6. **DON'T BE A FIXER.**
   The Bible says to confess our sins to each other, not to fix each other. The Spirit must work with the person to achieve change.

7. **ENCOURAGE THE CONFESSOR.**
   Thank the person for taking a risk and sharing what is going on. Express your gratitude for the courage it takes to confess sins.

8. **DON'T MAKE IT MANDATORY.**
   A group that forces everyone to confess is spiritually abusive. Each member is free to confess or not confess.

9. **BE AWARE.**
   In very rare instances, the confession of sin may involve the confession of a crime. Crimes against minors must be reported to the authorities. You can be held accountable if you don't report the abuse of a child.

5 Things that Shouldn't Be Shared in Groups

Some topics should not enter the conversation of a group. These topics are extremely difficult to navigate without veering into sin. As the old saying goes, "Some things are best left unsaid." If these topics come up, either shut them down quickly or talk with the offender outside of the group and express your concerns. Rest assured, most topics are on the table for small groups, but these five aren't:

1. **GOSSIP.**
   Sharing private information about others without their consent is gossip. If you are not part of the issue, the problem, or the solution, you are not part of it and should avoid discussing it.

2. **LEADER BASHING.**
   Some think criticism of church leaders is a sport, but the Bible warns us against such behavior (see Titus 3:1–11). If someone in your group voices concern or displeasure about a church leader, direct him or her to speak with that leader.

3. **CHURCH BASHING.**
   It's typical after a person has a bad experience with a past church, denomination, or religion to criticize it, but that helps no one. Honest evaluation is one thing, but bashing is another. If it's not helpful, it's not worth discussing.

4. **SEXUAL HISTORY.**
   We live in a very sexual cultural where private practices have entered public conversations. Unless you are in a support group or confessing sin in a gender-specific group, however, conversations about sexual experiences should be avoided.

5. **STRONGLY HELD PERSONAL OPINIONS ABOUT NON-ESSENTIAL MATTERS.**
We all have opinions about many things—but when we enter community we quiet those opinions out of respect for others. A wise person discerns between the essential and the non-essential and clings only to the essential. For centuries, documents such as the Apostle's Creed have outlined the simple "essentials." For instance, the belief that Jesus will return is essential, but how and when is non-essential. In other words, all Christians agree that he will return, but we may disagree on how and when. If you have questions about a particular issue, seek input from your pastor or coach.

Bible Study Principles for Every Small Group

A healthy small group explores biblical truth together. This requires applying good principles of biblical interpretation and application. Here are a few key principles:

1. **THE FINAL WORD.**
   The Bible is the authority. Sermons from great preachers, quotes from influential authors, and wisdom from various media personalities can be helpful and contribute to a good discussion. But God has the final word through his Word.

2. **CONTEXT IS KING.**
   If you take the "text" out of "context" you are left with a "con." Read Scripture in its context (not just isolated verses, but the verses that come before and after) to grasp the meaning.

3. **AUTHOR AND AUDIENCE.**
   What a biblical text meant to the author and the original audience is what it means. We can't make the text say what it was never intended to communicate.

4. **INTERPRET UNCLEAR WITH THE CLEAR.**
   When your group encounters a passage of Scripture that's difficult to understand or seems contradictory to other Scripture, use the clear texts to help shed light onto the less clear texts.

5. **SUBMIT TO SCRIPTURE.**
   Inevitably we will read something in the Bible that steps on our toes. Instead of ignoring it or changing the meaning to suit our interests, we need to submit to God's Word.

Use Curriculum Well

One of the most important tools that groups use is good curriculum. Curriculum is the material you use to guide the discussion. Videos, booklets, and questions written on a print-out are all examples of curriculum. If a group uses nothing but the Bible, the curriculum is the questions that form in their heads. No matter what you use, how you use it matters. Here are tips on making the best use of curriculum:

1. **CHOOSE CURRICULUM WITH LITTLE OR NO HOMEWORK.**
   Most group participants won't read a book, a chapter of a book, or watch a video before they come to the group. Look for material that can be completed within the group meeting time. The exception is the group built around set material that expects preparation work. This is a fine option for the group that embraces it. However, many group members might initially say they are open to homework but within weeks fail to follow through.

2. **LOOK FOR CURRICULUM THAT PROMOTES DISCUSSION AND ENCOURAGES PARTICIPATION.**
   If the material has a video, make sure the video doesn't take up more than 25-30 percent of the group time. It's no fun to spend all your time together silently watching a video.

3. **PRAY AND READ THROUGH THE MATERIAL BEFORE THE MEETING.**
   Ask God what he wants to reveal to your group members and where he wants growth. Also, read through the questions beforehand and make sure they make sense for your group.

4. **REWRITE AND ADAPT QUESTIONS TO FIT YOUR GROUP.**
   Since all study questions are for a general audience, don't be afraid to customize, edit, add, or eliminate questions so they fit your group.

5. **DON'T FEEL FORCED TO FINISH.**
   You are not obligated to answer all the questions each meeting. The purpose of the discussion isn't to learn more information about God, but to become more like him. Use the questions as a launching pad toward that goal.

5 Kinds of Curriculum to Avoid

Every group is unique, and all have different curriculum needs. That said, there are a few topics that won't work well in most groups. They are either too tough, require too much prior knowledge, or are too controversial for the average group to tackle. Your group members will either get lost in the material or constantly argue about personal experiences and opinions. Here are five topics to steer clear of:

1. **END TIMES.**
   In the 1970s, many churches tackled the topic, but instead of knowing the book of Revelation better, personal opinions and debates dominated the landscape. Even Jesus said that no man knows the hour or the date (Matthew 24:36). Leave behind the *Left Behind* series. It can lead to speculation, confusion, and division.

2. **FORMATION OF THE WORLD.**
   Good Christians have different interpretations of how God made the world and how long he took to make it. Did God make it in 6 literal 24-hour days, or did he take millions of years (or longer)? If your group can study creation without getting into a debate, go for it. But if it opens up passionate debate and hurtful division, it's best to choose another topic.

3. **TECHNICAL THEOLOGY.**
   Pneumatology, Soteriology, and Christology refer to technical theology around a specific topic with lots of people in different camps of thought. They are important and worthy of deep study, but the average small group will drown.

4. **CONTROVERSIAL TOPICS.**
   These topics change over time, but anything that sparks an argument and calls for speculation shouldn't be the topic of a small-group study.

5. **STUDIES CONTRARY TO YOUR CHURCH'S TEACHING.**
   Each denomination (and church) has its foundational
   doctrines. Groups should avoid topics that teach doctrine
   contrary to the leadership of their church unless they have
   received encouragement to do so from their pastor.

Curriculum Most Groups Will Enjoy

All groups thrive when the material they use engages their hearts, minds, and souls. Here's what to look for when choosing a study:

1. **PRACTICAL.**
   There is a reason the book of James is a small group favorite—it's very practical. Studies that have clear application hit the sweet spot for small groups.

2. **RELATIONAL.**
   Topics that help group members engage in healthy relationships are helpful. The Bible has a lot to teach about friendship, marriage, singleness, and parenting, and many groups find such studies engaging.

3. **ACCESSIBLE.**
   Simple studies that don't require deep study or advanced degrees are perfect for the typical small group. This doesn't mean that they don't require thought, or that the questions are overly simplistic, but that they're accessible to a wide range of people.

4. **INCLUSIVE.**
   Group members love studies that draw out each member and encourage everyone to interact. Material that only interests a select few in the group should be avoided.

5. **ONE BOOK.**
   It's easier for a small group to focus on one book of the Bible rather than jump around between passages. People who struggle to navigate the Bible feel more comfortable if they stay in one section and get to know that one book.

6. **NO HOMEWORK.**
   Very few group members will actually do the assigned home-work, so steer clear of any study that expects prep work.

Get the Off-Track Group Back on Track

Every group has the potential to drift from the main point of a Bible study or book discussion. Sometimes a group gets lost in a discussion that has no bearing on the lesson. Worse yet, sometimes groups shift into unbiblical solutions. Here are some things that can help when you get off track:

1. **HOIST THE FLAG.**
   Sometimes you just need to help group members recognize that they're heading down a rabbit trail that might get everyone lost. That alone can get the group back on track.

2. **GET A COMPASS AND A MAP.**
   Bring the group back to the discussion guide or curriculum, or return to the biblical text.

3. **IDENTIFY THE ULTIMATE AUTHORITY.**
   In our culture of strong opinions, bring your group back to the Bible and remind them that God's Word has final say. Others may be inspiring, but the Bible is inspired. If you need backup on this point, take the group to Psalm 119, 2 Timothy 3:16, and 2 Peter 1:20–21.

4. **KEEP THE MAIN THING THE MAIN THING.**
   As the old saying goes, in essentials there should be unity, in non-essentials liberty, and in everything love. As the group meanders, identify what is essential and what is non-essential. For centuries, documents such as the Apostle's Creed have outlined the simple "essentials." For instance, the belief that Jesus will return is essential, but how and when is non-essential. In other words, all Christians agree that he will return, but we may disagree on how and when. Each church identifies its essentials, so as a leader, be familiar with that list. When in doubt, seek wisdom from your coach or pastor.

5. **PHONE A FRIEND.**
   If the group gets into a serious gray area, call your coach or pastor for input. Or invite your coach to attend your next meeting to answer questions.

Set Personal Spiritual Goals

We can only hit the target we choose. If we don't choose any target, that's exactly what we will hit—nothing. But developing personal spiritual goals doesn't have to be intimidating. Here are some ways to get the creative ideas flowing:

1. **FIVE YEARS FROM NOW.**
   Picture your faith five years from now. What's your relationship with God like? What do you know and feel five years from now that you don't currently know or feel? What would it take to make that picture a reality?

2. **DESCRIBE ME.**
   How do you want this group to describe you? What do you want them to say about you?

3. **THE EPITAPH.**
   What do you wish your loved ones would write on your headstone? Is that true now? What can you do to live up to that description?

4. **TEAM EFFORT.**
   What is one thing our group could do that would help you grow in your relationship with God in the next six months?

5. **THE BARRIER.**
   What is holding you back? What are one or two barriers that keep you from growing in your walk with God? What are you willing to do about that?

Conduct a Great Prayer Time

Every healthy small group prays together. A great prayer time can open members up as they share deep and personal joys and pains. How do you make the most of this time? How do you avoid insincere and irrelevant prayer requests? Here are some suggestions:

1. **CARVE OUT ENOUGH TIME FOR PRAYER.**
   New groups might only need 5 minutes, while a group that's been together for several months might need 10 or 15. A group that's been together for a couple of years might take 30 minutes or more.

2. **LAY DOWN GUIDELINES.**
   Requests should be personally meaningful to the requester and rich in detail. We shouldn't spend group prayer time praying for an unnamed friend of a group member's coworker. "Unspoken" prayer requests should be left unspoken— they only lead to speculation and gossip.

3. **WRITE REQUESTS DOWN.**
   Ask a member of the group to volunteer to keep the group prayer journal and have him or her email the requests out to the group.

4. **AFFIRM CONFIDENTIALITY.**
   Remind the group that what is spoken in the group should stay within the group.

5. **PRAY.**
   Ask one person to offer a prayer over all the requests, recognizing God's presence during the request time and asking his blessing over the items shared. This doesn't have to be long. Remember that the act of sharing requests is in itself a prayer (see Matthew 18:20). Because God is present in Spirit, it's not necessary to repeat everything that was just shared.

7 Creative Ways to Improve Prayer Time

Some groups spend up to a quarter of their meeting time praying together or discussing prayer requests. Such a time priority means we need to lead the prayer time well. Here are some ideas to keep it fresh:

1. **SENTENCE PRAYERS.**
   Each person in the group can pray as he or she feels led, but each prayer can only be one sentence long. The group can pray as long as you like, and members can pray more than once so long as each prayer is one sentence.

2. **DIVIDE AND PRAY.**
   Split the group up into smaller groups of two or three. Each circle shares requests and prays together.

3. **WRITE IT DOWN.**
   Rather than pray as a group, pass out index cards and invite each person to write down a request. Then swap cards and challenge everyone to pray for the request on the card every day until you meet again.

4. **PRAISES ONLY.**
   Instead of sharing prayer requests, spend time in prayer thanking God for who he is and what he's done.

5. **PRAY SCRIPTURE.**
   Select a psalm or other passage of Scripture and pray it aloud.

6. **REPHRASE THE PSALMS.**
   Take a psalm and invite the group to put it in their own words. Divide up the stanzas and assign each one to an individual or smaller group within your group. Then pray through your paraphrased psalm.

7. **PRAY THROUGH A WORSHIP SONG OR HYMN.**
   Select a song or two and pray it—don't sing it. If your group is particularly musical, then sing it after you've prayed it.

Help People Grow Outside of Meetings

I f your group meets twice a month for 2 hours each time, then you have 48 hours in a year to help each person grow. You have a lot more time than that if you encourage your group members to use the time outside of the group meetings to grow in their faith. Here are some suggestions:

1. **ENCOURAGE EVERYONE TO ATTEND CHURCH REGULARLY.**
   Few Christians attend church regularly. Set an example and encourage all group members to go to church often—maybe even sit together. Make this a point of conversation within your group.

2. **ENCOURAGE EVERYONE TO HAVE A PERSONAL DEVOTIONAL TIME.**
   Model this by sharing the impact your personal devotional time has had on you. Encourage the daily reading of Scripture.

3. **SHARE GOOD RESOURCES.**
   Are you impacted by a particular podcast or book? Share it. Are you enjoying a new worship album? Recommend it.

4. **CHALLENGE EVERY GROUP MEMBER TO COMMIT TO AN AREA OF SERVICE.**
   Most of us grow in our love of Jesus as we learn to faithfully and selflessly serve the people that Jesus loves.

5. **ATTEND SPECIAL CHURCH EVENTS AS A GROUP.**
   If your church has extra growth opportunities, turn them into a group date and enjoy.

Find Future Leaders

We often fail to see the budding potential leaders right under our noses. What should we look for in potential leaders? (When you're ready to develop them, turn to page 127.)

1. **SPIRITUALLY VIBRANT.**
   Listen for group members who talk passionately about their relationship with God. Usually they will talk about what they are learning from Bible reading and other great books. Often, they digest worship music and are looking for different ways to grow in their relationship with God.

2. **GOOD REPUTATION.**
   Look for individuals that are seeking to honor God by making wise, godly choices that are consistent with a biblical lifestyle. They are the first to say they aren't perfect—but they are growing.

3. **AN INCLUDER.**
   Watch for group members who take an active interest in other people. They listen to others and want others to participate. They have an eye for the less-connected and draw them in. They may not be the life of the party, but they make sure everyone is enjoying the party.

4. **A SERVANT.**
   Look for people who are always willing to lend a hand and volunteer their time.

5. **GOOD WITH PEOPLE.**
   Watch for the person with solid interpersonal skills who is sensitive to the relationship dynamics in the group.

Develop Future Leaders

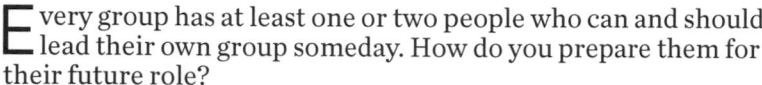

Every group has at least one or two people who can and should lead their own group someday. How do you prepare them for their future role?

1. **PRAY FOR THEM.**
   Throughout the Bible, leaders turned to God to help them identify and develop future leaders. Begin with a conversation with God.

2. **TALK TO YOUR COACH.**
   Ask your pastor or coach for suggestions on preparing these future leaders.

3. **ENCOURAGE THEM.**
   Tell them what you see in them and affirm them along the way.

4. **WORK THROUGH THEIR RESISTANCE.**
   They will probably say, "No, I could never lead a group!" You probably said the same thing at one time—confidently keep encouraging them forward.

5. **GIVE THEM RESPONSIBILITIES.**
   Ask them to lead the discussion or have them coordinate a service project or a special gathering. Let them carry part of the leadership load. Then encourage and coach them afterward.

6. **INVITE THEM TO GROWTH OPPORTUNITIES.**
   If you have a leader meeting or a meeting with your coach or pastor, bring them along.

7. **SPEND ADDITIONAL TIME WITH POTENTIAL LEADERS.**
   They don't care how much you know until they know how much you care. Get to know them as individuals and build them up.

8. **GIVE THEM HELPFUL RESOURCES.**
   Books, blogs, podcasts, and articles are great tools to develop leaders. Share with them what you have found helpful.

9. **ASK THE WHOLE GROUP TO ENCOURAGE POTENTIAL LEADERS.**
   Invite group members to affirm and encourage them.

10. **KEEP PRAYING FOR THEM AS THEY EXPLORE AND EMBRACE LEADERSHIP.**
    Leading a group is a spiritual endeavor—so appeal to God.

Section Four:
Cultivate a Heart for Others

4 Questions to Evaluate Your Heart for Others

Our concern for others is a key indicator of our spiritual maturity. As we pursue Christlikeness, we will see an increase in our passion for others. A key to shepherding our group members is discerning their heart for others. Here are some questions to help you evaluate:

1. **WHAT ARE YOU PRAYING ABOUT?**
   If all the prayer requests are of a personal nature (health, finances, relationships) and none are for friends without Christ, missions, or people you're serving, your group members probably need to develop a heart for others.

2. **HOW MANY PEOPLE IN YOUR GROUP ARE COMMITTED TO AN AREA OF SERVICE?**
   Many groups never serve together, and that's okay. But are group members engaged in service on their own—whether inside or outside the church?

3. **WHAT STORIES ARE BEING TOLD IN THE GROUP?**
   A group with a missional heart regularly swaps stories of the impact God is having on people around them.

4. **HOW DOES YOUR GROUP RESPOND WHEN PRESENTED WITH A NEED?**
   Do members step up and offer to help, or do they make excuses and hope someone else steps in?

Develop a Missional Group without Leaving the Family Room

It's a mistake to assume the only way a group can be missional is by leaving the meeting space. Certainly "going" is part of living a missional life. A healthy group, however, can accelerate their heart for others within their group meeting time. Here's how:

1. **STUDY GOD'S MISSION IN THE BIBLE.**
   Study passages where Jesus interacts with hurting, needy people. Start with the Great Commission (Matthew 28:18–20) and study the missionary work of Paul in the book of Acts.

2. **KEEP A LIST.**
   Challenge each group member to identify key people in their life who they want to invite to church or engage in a spiritual conversation.

3. **ADOPT A MINISTRY INSIDE THE CHURCH.**
   Ask a group member to communicate regularly with a ministry leader to stay up-to-date on needs and prayer concerns for that ministry (e.g., middle school small groups or Sunday toddlers) and commit as a group to praying for that ministry.

4. **ADOPT A MINISTRY OUTSIDE THE CHURCH.**
   Most churches partner with local Christian organizations. Identify one and pray for that ministry regularly.

5. **ADOPT A MISSIONARY.**
   Appoint a person in the group to regularly communicate with a missionary your church supports and pray for his or her needs every time you meet. When the missionary visits the area, invite him or her to your group.

6. **ADOPT A NATION OR REGION OF THE GLOBE.**
   Regularly dedicate group time to discuss and pray for the needs of that nation. Seek out news on that country or part of

the world and get updates on key stories. Create a discussion space via email or social media to discuss what you're learning to enhance your normal group discussions.

7. **BECOME A SEEKER GROUP.**
Add extra chairs and purposely seek out those who are spiritually seeking. Invite them to join your group, and patiently walk beside them on a journey of spiritual discovery.

Be Missional Outside of Meetings

Your group can have a great impact when you serve together. Consider these ideas for impacting your church or community:

1. **SERVE TOGETHER AT CHURCH.**
   Contact your coach or pastor and ask where your group could be useful in your church. Start with a one-time service opportunity, like cleaning the nursery or weeding a flower bed. Then consider a longer-term commitment.

2. **SERVE IN THE COMMUNITY.**
   Find a local ministry and volunteer together on a Saturday morning. Your group might fall in love with an area of ministry and begin a regular act of service.

3. **GO ON A PRAYER WALK.**
   Identify an area of town, meet as a group at a pre-selected location, split into smaller groups, and walk and pray together. The prayers don't need to be more profound than, "God help the people of this area," or "God, meet the needs of the people who work at this business." Talk to God as you walk along—it might seem awkward at first, but you'll adjust. Cap it off at a local coffee shop and share highlights from the experience.

4. **GO ON A MISSION TRIP TOGETHER.**
   This might seem like an advanced goal, but groups that serve on a mission trip together come back bonded and forever changed.

Why Your Group Should Serve Together

S mall groups benefit from the occasional serving opportunity. Here's why:

1. **IT'S BONDING.**
   Groups that serve together often build tighter connections with each other. By serving together, you create shared memories and experiences that you celebrate (and even laugh about).

2. **IT'S BIBLICAL.**
   Groups that show concern for those in need emulate the ministry of Jesus, who met spiritual and physical needs.

3. **IT'S BOLSTERING.**
   Serving strengthens everyone as you step outside your comfort zones and learn to help others. Service is a muscle that needs to be developed and exercised.

4. **IT'S BENEFICIAL.**
   Groups that do the same thing over and over atrophy. Groups that mix up the format of the group stay healthier longer.

Plan an Excellent Group Serving Opportunity

G roups that have a great experience serving together are more likely to repeat it. Here are some tips for planning an excellent serving opportunity:

1. **SET THE EXPECTATIONS.**
   How many hours? What type of work? Who will be involved? Where will we go? Will you meet and ride together, or just meet at the location? What time will you meet? When will you be finished? Answer these questions ahead of time. Ambiguity is the enemy of excellence.

2. **INVOLVE EVERYONE.**
   Serving as a spectator is no fun, so make sure that everyone has a chance to participate as their gifts and abilities allow.

3. **LOOK FOR A FIT.**
   With the time allowed and the abilities represented in the group, what are the opportunities available? If everyone is "all thumbs," helping build a Habitat for Humanity House is out, but sorting donations at Salvation Army might be perfect.

4. **BE FLEXIBLE.**
   Inevitably things change or differ from expectations, so instruct the group to accept those changes with grace.

5. **PRAY.**
   Before you begin, circle up with your group and pray.

6. **CELEBRATE TOGETHER.**
   After the opportunity is over, go out for dinner or coffee and celebrate the time of service. Alternatively, celebrate and debrief during your next group meeting.

Section Five:
Discover Biblical
Foundations for
Small Groups

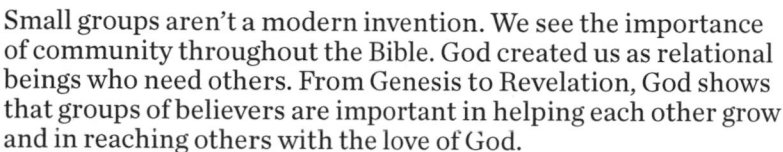

Small groups aren't a modern invention. We see the importance of community throughout the Bible. God created us as relational beings who need others. From Genesis to Revelation, God shows that groups of believers are important in helping each other grow and in reaching others with the love of God.

Principles of Community Life in the Old Testament

Sometimes we think that groups were invented in the New Testament. However, throughout the Old Testament, we see examples of the importance of community.

- We are made in the Image of God, who is three in one; this means that we are created with a deep need for others (Genesis 1 & 2).
- Jethro encouraged Moses to recruit and appoint leaders of the people to manage issues through a small-group-like system (Exodus 18).
- Moses was surrounded by a small group comprised of Aaron and Joshua as he led the nation (Exodus).
- David was surrounded by dozens of Mighty Men (2 Samuel 23:8–39).
- David said that when we experience unity, it's like a worship experience in the Temple. It's refreshing (Psalm 133).
- In his discouragement, God sent Elisha to Elijah as a partner, supporter, and encourager (1 Kings 19).

Principles of Community Life in Jesus' Teaching

A s God Incarnate, Jesus could have simply implanted his ideas into the minds and hearts of everyone. Instead, he modeled a relationally rich connection. Here are just a few examples:

- He chose to invite the 12 to be with him and to learn from him (Mark 3:14).
- He demonstrated and communicated the importance of reaching out to others (Matthew 9:37–38).
- He taught how to develop healthy community by avoiding gossip and employing godly confrontation (Matthew 18).
- He modeled selfless service and challenged his followers to serve one another in similar fashion (John 13).
- As he reinstated Peter, Jesus communicated that love for him is shown in how we build up other followers (John 21).

Principles of Community Life in Paul's Letters

The apostle Paul wrote extensively to small groups of believers in towns across the Roman Empire. Many of these churches functioned like small groups—gathering regularly in homes, sharing life, and studying God's Word together. What did Paul tell these groups to do?

- In love, show devotion to one another (Romans 12:10).
- Seek harmony in your community (Romans 12:16).
- Don't be judgmental of one another (Romans 14:13).
- Encourage one another to learn and teach each other (Romans 15:14).
- Take interest in one another (1 Corinthians 12:25).
- Look for opportunities to serve one another (Galatians 5:13).
- Confront one another lovingly (Galatians 6:1).
- Demonstrate support for one another in tangible and emotional ways (Galatians 6:2).
- Build one another up using spiritual resources (Ephesians 5:19).
- Be willing to put your ideas second (Ephesians 5:21).
- God started the work in his community and will finish what he starts (Philippians 1:6).
- Willingly forgive one another (Colossians 3:13).
- Take the risk to challenge on another to pursue godliness (Colossians 3:16).
- Encourage one another (1 Thessalonians 5:11).
- Build one another up (1 Thessalonians 5:11).

Principles of Community Life in Other New Testament Literature

Jesus modeled groups and Paul taught on groups, but it didn't end there. James, Jude, Peter, John, and the mystery author of Hebrews also wrote of the impact the Christian community can have:

- Daily look for opportunities to encourage others (Hebrews 3:13).
- Spur one another on toward love and good deeds (Hebrews 10:24).
- Refuse to gossip or slander others (James 4:11).
- Don't complain about or criticize one another (James 5:9).
- Confess sins to close friends in your community (James 5:16).
- Lift one another up in prayer (James 5:16).
- Genuinely love one another deeply, from the core of your being (1 Peter 3:8; 1 Peter 4:8).
- Seek unity (1 Peter 3:8).
- Open up your house and share meals without complaining (1 Peter 4:9).
- Use the spiritual gifts God has given you to serve others (1 Peter 4:10).
- Be humble in your interactions and put the needs of others before your own (1 Peter 5:5).
- Genuinely and truly love one another (1 John 4:7–21).
- Patiently journey with the doubters and skeptics in your community (Jude 22).
- Love others without embracing their sin (Jude 23).
- Through John, Jesus sent messages to seven churches encouraging, admonishing, and correcting these communities of people to pursue faithfulness to God and proper relationships with one another (Revelation 1–3).

SmallGroups.com provides everything you need for a healthy, thriving small-group ministry. With 100+ training tools, 800+ Bible studies, and thousands of articles, we're your go-to resource for all things small groups. Find the small-group model that's right for your ministry, develop a group strategy, organize your ministry details, start and manage a coaching system, recruit and train leaders with our innovative resources, and troubleshoot common group issues. Visit SmallGroups.com today.

Made in the USA
San Bernardino, CA
29 June 2019